Sudantha Gunawardena

Design Principles and Usability

Human Computer Interaction

GRIN Publishing

Bibliographic information published by the German National Library:

The German National Library lists this publication in the National Bibliography; detailed bibliographic data are available on the Internet at http://dnb.dnb.de .

Imprint:

Copyright © 2010 GRIN Verlag GmbH
Print and binding: Books on Demand GmbH, Norderstedt Germany
ISBN: 978-3-640-92034-1

This book at GRIN:

http://www.grin.com/en/e-book/172251/design-principles-and-usability

GRIN - Your knowledge has value

Since its foundation in 1998, GRIN has specialized in publishing academic texts by students, college teachers and other academics as e-book and printed book. The website www.grin.com is an ideal platform for presenting term papers, final papers, scientific essays, dissertations and specialist books.

Visit us on the internet:

http://www.grin.com/

http://www.facebook.com/grincom

http://www.twitter.com/grin_com

Human Computer Interaction

Design Principles and Usability

Sudantha Gunawardena

Asia Pacific Institute of Information Technology

Sri-Lanka

8th February 2010

Design principles and guidelines

According to Pop,P(2001,p.13)defines that design principles is 'high level' recommendations based on well established knowledge about human behavior.

Ryan(c. 2009) clarify that many of these design principles has been concerned in design of computer interfaces like Microsoft Windows and Mac operation system these guide lines will make program interfaces easier to use but some of these recommendations may not relevant to web applications.

According to Spring (2004) highlights that there are various set of design guidelines has been introduced by various people.

Introducer	Principles / rules
Shneiderman	3 Principles , 8 golden rules
Norman	7 principles
Borenstien	10 commandments
Mandel	3 golden rules
Johnson	9 principles,82 bloopers

Table 1

But mainly principles and rules which are introduced by Shneiderman and Norman are popular and used in practice widely.

Ben Shneiderman

University of Maryland (2009) states that Ben Sheinerman is a professor in the department of computer science and the founder of the Human computer interaction laboratory in university of Maryland.

Also according to University of Maryland (2009) Dr.Shendierman is a author for many research papers in human computer interaction.

8 Golden rules of Ben Shneiderman

University of Washington(2009) defines that there are 8 rules proposed by Shneiderman and most of the rules are applicable to most of the interactive systems including web applications and guiding this rules the usability can be improved in software applications..

1. Strive for consistency

2. Enable frequent users to use shortcuts

3. Offer informative feedback

4. Design dialogs to yield closure

5. Offer error prevention and simple error handling

6. Permit easy reversal of actions

7. Support internal locus of control

8. Reduce short-term memory load

Design Principles and Usability

Strive for consistency

According to Shniederman(1998) as he highlighted that strive for consistency means consistent sequences of actions should be required in similar scenarios and use of identical terminology should be used in message boxes , forms and windows.

As described in Beckert & Beuster (2006,p. 22) we will take a text based e-mail application as an example for consistency.

Screen 1

Figure 2 – Idle screen of the mailSource :Beckert&Beuster (2006,p. 22)

Design Principles and Usability

Screen 1

```
Result of latest command:  No new email arrived
------------------------------------------------------------------




edit (m)ail | (s)end mail | (f)etch mail
```

Figure 3 – Screen 2 Source :Beckert & Beuster (2006,p. 22)

As above figures the menu is the bottom of the screen is constant for every screen in the application.

By consistency the interface users can easily understand the elements in the application

Design Principles and Usability

The following figure shows Microsoft office 2007 ribbon bar asan example for consistency .All the tools can be accessed as tabs.

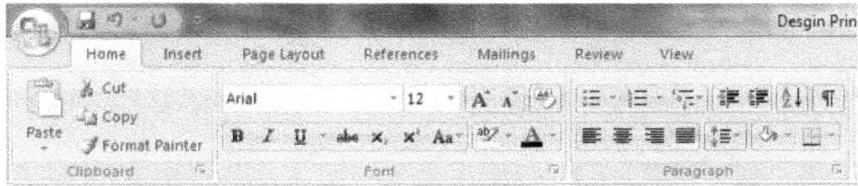

Figure 4 – Ribbon bar in Microsoft Office(Source: Microsoft Office)

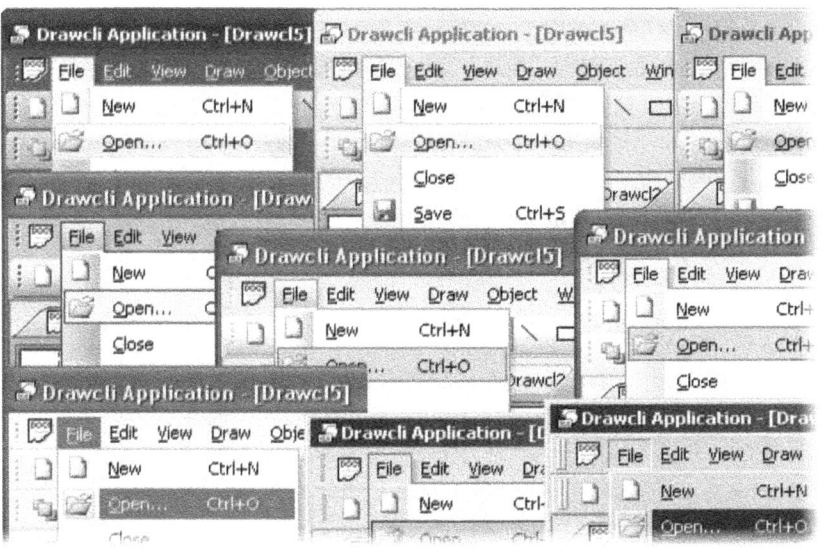

Figure 5 - consistency in Microsoft windows applications(Source: Microsoft Windows)

The above figure shows some windows of software applications the menu bar, toolbar, can be clarified as consist objects so user can easily identify.

Design Principles and Usability

Enable shortcuts for frequent users

As Pop, P (2001, p.22) defines shortcuts may advantage frequent users to do their tasks easily .shortcuts can be implemented in several ways like,

- Keyboard shortcuts
- Special menus
- Special Keys and icons
- Macros

Especially keyboard shortcuts and menus are frequently used in most of the applications and macros are pre recoded instructions which can be used instantly.

According to Microsoft Corporation(2002) 'Official Guidelines for User Interface Developers and Designers ' p.76 highlight there are many shortcuts are used in Microsoft Windows graphical user interface, like double-clicking with the primary mouse button is a shortcut for the operation of an object.

Keyboard Shortcuts

Also as Microsoft Corporation (2002) 'Official Guidelines for User Interface Developers and Designers' p.82 describes there are many keyboard shortcut techniques are used, for example to get help the default key is the F1 key and to close a windows the shortcut key combination is ALT + F4.Also custom software application may have customized keyboard shortcuts in use .

Design Principles and Usability

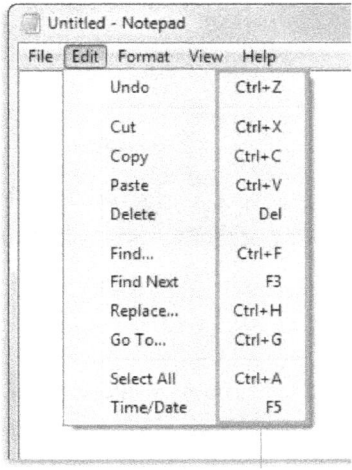

Figure 6 - Keyboard Shortcuts(Source: Microsoft Windows)

Buttons and Menus

According to Microsoft(2009) in Microsoft corporation have introduced new concepts on Windows 7 taskbar which will provide quick access to programs and quick access to frequent tasks .

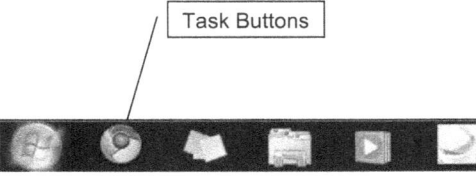

Figure 7 - Taskbar in Windows 7(Source: Microsoft Windows)

Design Principles and Usability

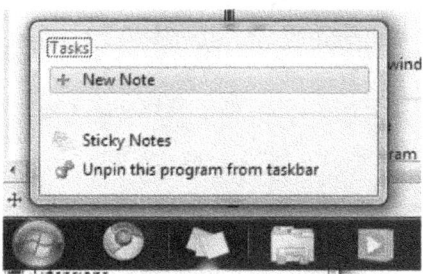

Figure 8 - Shortcut menu associated with the Task buttons(Source: Microsoft Windows)

As figure above shows task buttons provide shortcuts to frequently used programs and the newly introduced the shortcut menu which is associated with taskbar provides access more specifically. And these shortcuts are provided automatically as the frequent of use or user can customize the shortcuts.

Macros

Also in 90's macros was a popular way of doing tasks easily .Pre-configured set of tasks will run when user requested or these tasks can be customized or generated by the user .but in modern days macros are not recommended to use because macro scripts have a high vulnerability of spreading viruses and spyware .

Special keys

The windows key is a special key ( ) which available in most of the keyboards which lead to shortcuts that can be used in Microsoft windows.

Design Principles and Usability

Icons

According to Windows help Icons are graphical representations of files, programs, users can easily memorize chunk of graphics, finding and access of the application may be faster.

Design Principles and Usability

Offer informative feedback

According to Pop, P (2001, p.23) describes for every user action there should be a system feedback. And make this feedback universal; designers can use visual representations like progress indicators.

As Microsoft Corporation (2002, p.185) defines the progress bar control is a one of the key progress indicators.

Figure 9 - Progress bar control (Source: Microsoft Windows)

As the above figure shows in Microsoft windows environment which can be easily identified like a consist of a solid or segmented rectangular bar that "fills" from left to right.

Except the progress bar control Slider bar control also can be used as a Feedback indicator.

Figure 10 – Slider bar(Source: Microsoft Windows)

Design Principles and Usability

Error control

Error prevention

According to Pop,P. (2001,p.26) remark that the software architects should design the software without any bugs so that users cannot make serious errors in the runtime .by doing this errors may be prevented and system will run without any interference.

Also Pop,P. (2001,p.26) describes further that when application need to take user data instead of using form fill-in interfaces designers can use graphical user objects like menus to gather data from the users. So errors which are occurred when data entering of user will be prevented.

Also in different scenarios designers can use validations on user enter data which will also prevent errors.

For example in a registration form is there a field to enter a telephone numbers designers should not allow alphabetic characters in this numeric field.

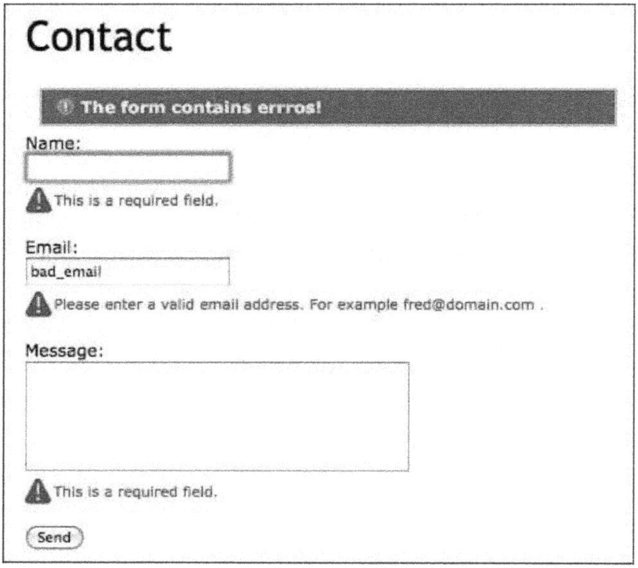

Figure 11 - Form validation in a web site, Source: Cristi(2009).

The above figure shows a web registration form which has proper error prevention and validation methods. If the fields are blank or wrong information is entered error is prevented and user is guided though a scenario which helps to recover the error.

Design Principles and Usability

Error handling

According to Pop, P. (2001,p.26) describes that error handling can be defined as in few steps

- What happened?
- Why did it happened?
- How serious is it?
- How can it be fixed?

In case of an error designers should not change the state of the system and handle the error in simple and constructive way and error details and specific instructions should be promoted using error messages.

Error Messages

Error message can be defined as a prompt to the user which error is occurred and which action that user can be involved in.

The following picture explains how to design proper error messengers in UI designing.

In the following example as Sommerville,I. (1999, p.74) explains in a hospital management system in a scenario which take a name of a patient and if the name is not found prompt a error message.

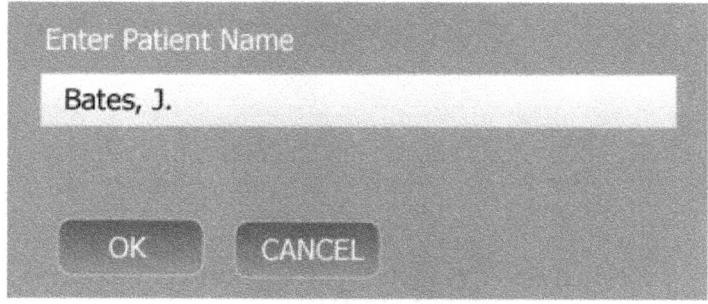

Figure 12 – Nurse input of a patient's name Source: Sommerville,I(1999, p.75)

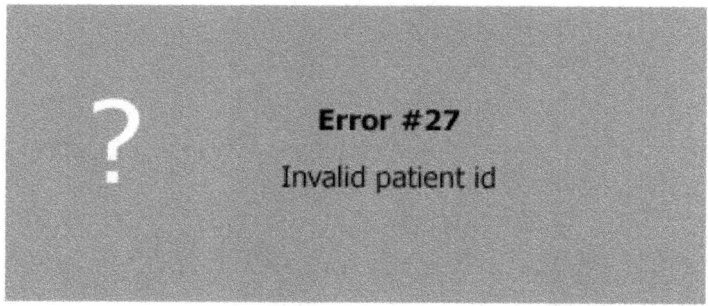

Figure 13 – A badly designed error message Source: Sommerville,I(1999, p.76)

The above figure shows a badly designed error message which user may be confused .the above error message does not has a mapping with the real world terms and used technical terms ,as nurses are less technical people it will be hard to understand ,also promoting the error ID which will be a irrelevant information.

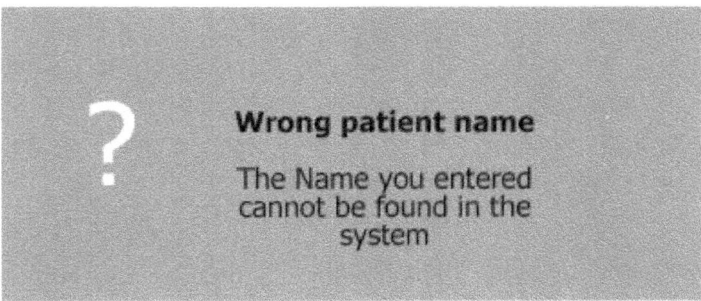

Figure 14 - A good designed error message Source: Sommerville,I(1999, p.76)

The above picture shows a proper design of an error message. The phrase has a mapping with the real world language, and non-technical users can easily understand.

Design Principles and Usability

Reduce short-term memory load

As the main goal of human computer interaction is to make the interfaces more user friendly .and there may be different kind of users which have different memory capacities using the same software so the interface designers should minimize the load of the memory on users and make them easier to use.

Types of Memory

Short Term Memory

According to Kristin, A. (2004, p.2) describes that short time memory is the working memory which keeps the temporary store that keeps the information active we are using or until we use it .

Short term memory can be can be explained using baddelay's working model of memory.

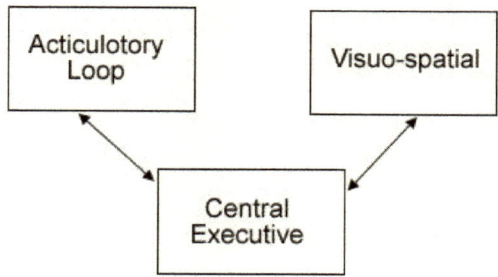

Figure 15 – Baddelay's Working model of short term memory Kristin, A (2004, p.3)

Design Principles and Usability

As Kristin, A. (2004, p.3) short term memory depends on several factors like capacity, attention of the person, confusability of the data.

Kristin, A. (2004, p.3) also reflects that an average human can remember 7 ±2chunks of information in generally.

To reduce short term memory load designers can concern on several design aspects like:

- Stick to the rules of short memory
- Keep display simple
- Online access to commands and codes.
- Train users for long sequence actions.

Permit easy reversal of actions

As Huang ,M(2009) confirms Permit easy reversal of actions can be simply define as 'undo ' .As user can undone the things he did so users can easily explore unfamiliar options and software .so new users can easily adapt to systems and use the systems without any stress.

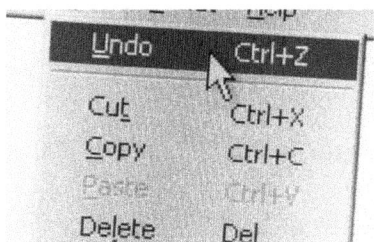

Figure 16 - Undo button in a menu: Source Virulent Word of Mouse (2008)

The above figure shows a menu of a software application that has reversal actions, if user needs to reverse any action he can use the menu item or for the power users can use keyboard shortcut, the common keyboard shortcut for undo command is CTRL + Z

Many applications have the reversal command available in most applications and to access to frequent user's keyboard shortcuts also available. But as a disadvantage is number of undo times are limited in most applications.

Expanding these idea developers has come up with various new technologies for example as Microsoft (2009) clams their tool 'System Restore' can undo user's system files to an earlier point in time.

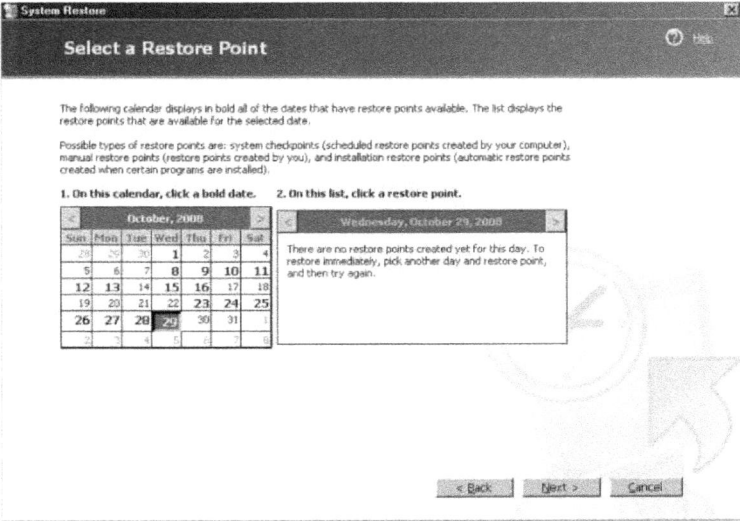

Figure 17 - System restore tool: CA Community (2009)

The above figure shows the system restore tool available in Microsoft windows operating system. If user does a wrong installation or change of settings and system is malfunctioning due to those reasons users can easily reverse their actions and restore the settings to anearlier time.

Modern application has redo actions also will help users to work with the new systems.

Design dialogs to yield closure

According to Carr, D (1995, p.5) describes that when developers designing every action sequences it should have a proper flow with a beginning, middle and an end.

For example a purchasing items via internet (amazon.com) has a clearly defined step by step process

Figure 18 - Checkout wizard in amazon.com Source: amazon.com(2009)

As above figure shows the internet shopping which is a sequence of actions which as a clear beginning which is 'sign in' and a clear end which is 'place order' has been defined properly.

With this layout as Carr, D (1995, p.12) clarify thatusers can easily understand the scope of there actions.

Support internal locus of control

According to Neill, J (2006) locus of control is an individual's idea about the main causes of events. In interface designing this perception will be an important aspect.

When a user interacts with the system usershould not be 'surprised' with actions he took or the reactions that the system has made.

Also as Pop,P(2001 p.32) claims locus of control will be loss when users have to do tiresome sequences of data entries, difficult to get the data user want to desire or user cannot make the action he need.

The following examples will show bad user interface design which will user will get surprised.

Design Principles and Usability

The following figure shows WinZIP software which is common software that uses to compress the files which is a really simple process. But prompting a wizard by asking irrelevant questions may irritate to the user.

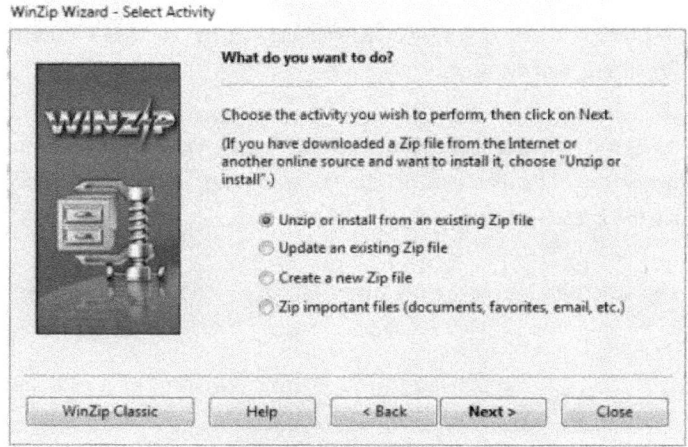

Figure 19 - WinZip Wizard Source: gHacks(2009)

Always designers should keep the user in charge of the interface and interface should rapidly response to the user without building anxiety and dissatisfactions in user.

Design Principles and Usability

Following figure shows an error message which can be found in Microsoft outlook5 express

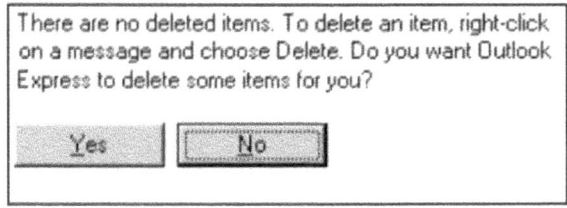

Figure 20 - Error message found in Microsoft outloock expresess Source : Pop,P(2001, p.34)

As this message describes that the application will delete randomly selected messages from Microsoft outlook express. Users may not be agreeing with deleting random messages from his emails and it's not a good usability practice.

Usability

According to Nielsen, J (1993) 'Usability' is a quality attribute that assesses how easy user interfaces are to use.

Also Quesebery, W (2001) clams that usability is defined in ISO 9241-11 standard is: The extent to which a product can be used by specified users to achieve specified goals with effectiveness, efficiency, and satisfactionSupport cost in a specified context of use.

Usability Principles and Concepts

Usability concepts by Nielsen

According to Maurizio, C (n.d, p.5) describes that Nelsen, J (1993) has identified five attributes of usability. The attributes can be described as follows.

- **Learnability**

    The user can able to perform his tasks from the application
- **Efficiency**

    When user is familiar with the system a high productivity should be possible
- **Memoability**

    Users should not be relearning anything again about the system.
- **Errors**

    There should be proper ways to recover from errors and catastrophic errors should not be occur

- **Satisfaction**

    System should satisfy users need and pleasant to use.

Don Norman's Usability Guidelines

According to Norman's Design principles there are 7 design principles proposed to make good usability design.

The principles are following

- Use existing knowledge
- Simplify tasks
- Increase visibility
- Present correct mappings
- Exploit constraints
- Designing for error
- Standardize controls and operations

Design Principles and Usability

According to Constantine, L (1994) describes more 6 principles in usability engineering. They can be defined as following.

- Structure
- Simplicity
- Visibility
- Feedback
- Tolerance
- Reuse

Structure principle

As Summerville,M(1999,p8) describes structure can be the organize of the interface peacefully and a meaningful manner .using this principles designers have are suggested to group the related things together .

Simplicity principle

According to Summerville,M(1999,p8) designers are advised to keep the interface simple. Also use of natural languages, shortcutsshould be used meaningfully.

Visibility principle

Summerville,M(1999,p8) claims that all options and materials on the application interface should visible and should not distracted to the user.

Feedback principle

User should be kept updated and informed about the state of the application same as Sheinerman's 3 golden rules.

Design Principles and Usability

Tolerance principle

According to Constantine, L (1994) describes tolerance principle reduces cost of making mistakes and misuse by reversal actions while preventing errors by tolerating various inputs

Reuse principle

Mainly Summerville, M(1999,p8) verify that this principle will helps to reduce the rethink of the users rethink ability while using the system. So the users do not need to rethink and do actions on the system.

Ten Usability Heuristics

The 'Ten Usability Heuristics' which published by Dr.Jakob Nielsen.

According to Nielsen, J. (c. 1990) there are 10 usability heuristics are defined and described as following.

1. **Visibility of system status**

    The application should be designed to keep updated the user in real time what's going on the application.

2. **Match between system and the real world**

    The application should not use any technical terms and proposed to use familiar phrases to the user which are used in real world conversations.

3. **User control and freedom**

    The user should have the freedom of the applications. Designers should give freedom to move windows as user wants skip several dialogs or customize the user interface.

4. **Consistency and standards**

    Windows, graphics and parses, buttons should be constant within the same application.

5. **Error prevention**

    As much as validations should be included in the application and application should be tested properly and ensure that no or few bugs are remain.

6. **Recognition rather than recall**

    Designers should consider actions, objects and options should be visible to the user. If there are several windows in the application the user should not need to remember information from one window to another window.

7. Flexibility and efficiency of use

Designers should consider about the user groups that the application will used. Expert user may have a speed interaction with the system and novice users may have slow interaction, so application should be flexible for these user groups.

8. Aesthetic and minimalist design

Windows should not contain any irrelevant information which is not needed to user actions and windows and dialogs should be contain with relevant information which help users to ease their actions.

9. Help users to recover from errors

If there any error messages prompts it should be clear and users must be guided which steps should be taken next.

10. Help and documentation

Application should be contain with proper documentation with guides that user can easily understand.

Web usability

According to Friedman,V(2008) there approximately 10 best practiced guide lines for effective web design which will be focused on heuristics and principles for effective web design.

- Don't make users think
- Don't squander users' patience
- Manage to focus users' attention
- Strive for feature exposure
- Make use of effective writing
- Strive for simplicity
- Don't be afraid of the white space
- Communicate effectively with a "visible language"
- Conventions are our friends
- Test early, test often

Don't make users think

Friedman,V(2008) describes that according to Krug(2000) the web page should be obvious to the user and should be self-understandable without user's have to think about the design and the content of the web application .

Design Principles and Usability

Don't squander users' patience

Friedman,V(2008) claims that if the developed web site provide any services by gaining user requirements or information designers should try to keep the user requirement minimal .if not user may be bored getting registering on your application before use it .

If we take many registration procedures in online some web sites has good registration options like with link with other services that user already register ,so user do not need to enter the same data again.

Manage to focus users' attention

If designers choose several multimedia objects on the web page like text, animation ,pictures every other multimedia objects than text has a high probability of eye catching of the user, so designers should manage the use of pictures and animations.

Strive for feature exposure

AsFriedman,V(2008) defines designers should provide the site content in a very simple readable effective way. If there any criteria with several steps, steps should be implemented in step by step in an effective way.

Make use of effective writing

When expression the site content and the text expressions designers should use clever ways to express it. for example as Friedman,V(2008) describes when user needs to create an account except of "sign up" better eye catching words like "start now !" can be used, these terminologies are used in real world languages also ,so users can easily understand.

Design Principles and Usability

Strive for simplicity

As always interfaces should be kept simple. According to several case studies only few of the internet users are rarely enjoining the design of the web site. Designers should keep the design strive for simplicity instead of complexity

Don't be afraid of the white space

According to Friedman,V(2008) when a new user approaches a website the user firstly he scan the page and divide the content area into pieces of information. So the information should be implemented in harder to read style.

Communicate effectively with a "visible language"

According toMarcus,A(1995) states that visible language refers to graphical techniques that used to communicate the content .all the graphics animations, icons, art can be consider as visible language.

Use of good visible language may be a key to a good usability desgin.

Conventions are our friends

The design element in the web page makes the web page interesting and eye catching to the user. According to Friedman,V(2008) that the use of conventions reduce the learning curve of the users, than means users do not need to specially figure out what to do in the web application

Design Principles and Usability

Test early, test often

According to Krug,S(2000) testing one user is 100% better than testing none, so testing is a critical stage in usability design. There are many ways usability testing can be done and a measure usability goal, testing leads systems to perfect.

Design Principles and Usability

ISO 9241-11 Guidance on Usability

Usability can be defined in several sub components variously as various research papers but according to Bevan, N (c.2008, p.2) usability components as defined in ISO 9241-11 as following as a standard.

- Usability
- Effectiveness
- Efficiency
- Satisfaction

As Bevan, N (2008, p.2) points out the ISO standard guidelines are following,

Usability – Ease of use

Effectiveness – The accuracy of user achieve specified goals

Efficiency – Relation to the accuracy which users achieve goals

Satisfaction – The comfort of the use.

Usability Goals/Requirements

When developing UI developers have to consider about usability, effectiveness, efficiency, satisfaction so the designers can gain many benefits and focus on the correct requirement of the user, identify customer characteristics and types of customers and provide good solutions to the customer.

According to Lindgaard, G (1993, p.254) usability goal can be defined as a statement which helps the design team to focus its efforts by defining what it is aiming for.

As Herr's, S (2007, p.5) describes archive these goals and requirements designers can consider about the following aspects in the UI designs by use of appropriate:

- Ascertain user's needs
- Ensure proper reliability
- Standardization
- Integration
- Consistency
- Portability

The advantage of using and setting usability goals is that the designers can measure the amount of success in the system and eliminate wrong design concepts and gain the user's needs.

Design Principles and Usability

Usability metrics

Church,R(1993,p.10) claimsthat there are many ways to collect usability metrics like

- Heuristic reviews
- Usability lab testing
- Surveys
- User reporting methods
- Benchmarking
- User attitude scales

Heuristic reviews

According to Church,R(1993,p.250) describes that heuristic reviews are a method of analyze the user interface by the design team .the design team should include usability design experts.

Usability lab testing

As Church,R(1993,p.250) claims lab testing is method of usability testing that observing a sample of users with the interaction of the system and report them in a proper way. Then the design teams come up with certain metrics like average errors, time user requested for help.

Surveys

Benchmarking

In modern computing benchmarking is a widely used technique. According to Church, R.(1993,p.252) defines benchmarking can be used in usability engineering to compare the interface with a another competitive product.

User attitude scales

Church, R.(1993,p.252) suggests most of the users make purchase decisions on perception that mean the attribute for the product .user attitude can be measured using normal usability tests and user attitude scales .

Measurable usability goals

According to usability.gov (2009) there is several usability goals that can be measurable, typical usability goals including

- Time
- Accuracy
- Satisfaction
- Success

Time

Designers can set various usability goals using the 'time' parameter

- Time to get the application startup
- Response time of an action
- The responding time when user do certain actions
- Time that user take to understand the system

Accuracy

Designers can set usability goals to measure accuracy by taking a time interval and give users to carry out several tasks in the application

- Number of errors occurred
- Number of unproductive searches
- Number of wrong navigation choices

Design Principles and Usability

Success

This usability goal is set to calculate the success on your application that users can perform their tasks and solve the problem using application and this goal can be extended to find how users will get to the success.

Satisfaction

This usability goal is set to find out does the users are happy with the system and find out the overall satisfaction in various functions in the system, so the designers can set several usability goals in sub functions in the system.

As Bevan, N (c.2008, p.10) clams different user types may have different goals from the same system or application. The following figure shows kind of user and how their goals are different from each other.

	End User	Usage Organization	Technical support
Main goal	Usability	Cost-effectiveness	Maintenance
Characteristics	Personal goals	Task goals	Support goals
System effectiveness	User effectiveness	Task effectiveness	Support effectiveness
System resources	Productivity	Cost efficiency	Support cost

So as our system is used my various user groups usability goals should be set to all these user groups ,If designers can gain these usability goals system will be efficient and reliable for the users,

Design Principles and Usability

Setting usability goals

To measure the successful usability level of our application we have we to set and test on usability goals. We proposed sample

- Successfully complete transactions in 2 minutes
- Pages will be loaded in 2seconds using a broadband connection.
- Recover from an error in a certain time
- Find the correct hardware details and specifications
- Rating for the site using start rating
- Desire to use the system in the future
- Make no more than 5 errors while using the system.
- Overall satisfaction rating by the user
- 40% users who use the web site will be place an order
- 90% users will able to find and click the specific link
- 90% users can able to work with visual representations like (combo boxes)
- Help disk system will able to answer the user problems in 2 hours

References

Beckert, B &Beuster,G 2006, *Guaranteeing consistency in text-based Human computer interaction*, University of Koblenz-Landau,

Bevan, N. c.2008.*UX, Usability and ISO Standards,*Professional Usability Services.
Carr, D. 1995. *Dialog Design:User Centered Design.* Luleå University.

Church,R 1993, *Measuring usability against usability goals during the product development cycle,*Hewlett-Packard Co,Portland.

Constantine, L 1994,Collaborative *Usability Inspections for Software. Software Development,*Miller Freeman,San Francisco.

Cristi 2009,*Radiant Mailer Extension basic usage.*[Online] 12 December 2009.Available from:blog.aissac.ro,http://blog.aissac.ro/2009/08/30/radiant-mailer-extension-client-side-validation. [Accessed: 15th January 2010].

Friedman,V 2008,*10 Principles of Effective Web Design,* Smashing Magazine.

Herr's, S. 2007. *Usability of Interactive Systems,* Chicago: Loyola University.

Huang, M 2009.*Design Principles.*[Online]. Available from:http://www.cc.gatech.edu/classes/cs6751_97_winter/Topics/design princ/[Accessed: 18 January 2010].

Kristin, A. 2004, *The Impact of Memory on HCI*, DePaul University,2005.

Krug,S 2000,*Usability testing on 10 cents a day,*PearsonEducation,United States.

Lindgaard, G. 1993.*Usability testing and system evaluation: a guide for designing useful computer systems*, England: Taylor & Francis.

Marcus,A 1995, *Principles of effective visual communication for graphical user interface design*,Morgan Kaufmann Publishers Inc,San Francisco.

Maurizio, C. n,d ,*Human-computer interaction and main principles to design practice Human centered system* ,Universitàdella Calabria, Italy.

Microsoft Corporation, 2002. *'Official Guidelines for User Interface Developers and Designers'.* Redmond: Microsoft Press.

Neill, J. 2006. *Psychology of Human Growth & Transpersonal Education*: Wilderdom.

Nielsen, J. 1993 .*Usability Engineering.* Academic Press Limited.

NVIDIA, 2009 *NVIDIA Speak Visual,* [Online].Available from: www.speakvisual.com[Accessed: 05 February 2010].

Pop, P 2001 *'Design Principles of HCI'*, Linkoping university.

Principles of HCI Design2004, *Proliferation of Principles*, [Online], http://benedict.cs.loyola.edu/CS774/cs774lecture5principles.pdf [Accessed: 21 December 2009].

Quesebery, W. 2001.*What Does Usability Mean: Looking Beyond 'Ease of Use'* [Online]. Available from: http://www.wqusability.com/articles/more-than-ease-of-use.html [Accessed: 14 January 2010].

Shniederman, B. 1998, *Designing for user interface: Strategies for effective human-computer interaction*, University of Maryland.

Sommerville, I. 1999, *Software Engineering,* Addison-Wesley, California.

Summerville, M 1999,*Web Interface Design Issues: Usability*, [Online]Available from:http://blacksunimages.com/usability/sld008.htm.[Accessed:3 February 2010]

University of Washington, 2009.*Shneiderman'sEight Golden Rules of Interface Design*. Washington: University Press.

Usability.gov2009,*Set Measurable Usability Goals* [Online].Available from:http://www.usability.gov/analyze/goals.html [Accessed: 05 February 2010].